Butterflies and Flowers Coloring Book for Adults

By Mindful Coloring Books

Copyright © 2018 by Mindful Coloring Books

All rights reserved. No part of this publication may be reproduced, distributed, or transmitted in any form or by any means, including photocopying, recording, or other electronic or mechanical methods.

Coloring Tips

~ Sometimes what you think the color will look like and what it will actually look like are very different. Use the color test page.

~ Don't press too hard. Start out coloring lightly and you can always go back and make it darker.

~ Keep your pencil tips sharp so you can get into all the intricate spaces.

~ Using markers? Place a scrap piece of paper behind the page you are coloring. Pages in this book are only printed on one side but there is still the risk of bleed through to the next page.

~ Try different coloring utensils marketed for adults. It is fun and quality can vary greatly.

COLOR TEST PAGE

COLOR TEST PAGE

Enjoy these preview pages from some of our other coloring books!

Beautiful Spring Scenes Coloring Book

Simple Flower and Vine Designs

Leave us a review on Amazon!

Mindful Coloring Books:

Coloring books for adults

Coloring books for kids

Journals

Notebooks

Planners

Check out
Mindful Coloring Books

www.mindfulcoloringfun.com

amazon.com/author/mindfulcoloringbooks

Free coloring pages on our Facebook page!

www.ingramcontent.com/pod-product-compliance
Lightning Source LLC
Chambersburg PA
CBHW081018240526
45471CB00017B/3410